Broke
BAROQUE

BOOKS BY TONY MEDINA

POETRY
Broke Baroque
An Onion of Wars
Broke on Ice
My Old Man Was Always on the Lam
Committed to Breathing
Sermons from the Smell of a Carcass Condemned to Begging
No Noose Is Good Noose
Emerge & See

FOR YOUNG READERS
The President Looks Like Me & Other Poems
I and I, Bob Marley
Follow-up Letters to Santa from Kids who Never Got a Response
Love to Langston
Christmas Makes Me Think
DeShawn Days

EDITOR
Role Call: A Generational Anthology of Social and Political Black Literature & Art, with Samiya A. Bashir and Quraysh Ali Lansana
Bum Rush the Page: A Def Poetry Jam, with Louis Reyes Rivera
In Defense of Mumia, with S. E. Anderson

Broke BAROQUE

by Tony Medina

With an Introduction by
Ishmael Reed

2LEAF PRESS

NEW YORK

www.2leafpress.org

P.O. Box 4378
Grand Central Station
New York, New York 10163-4378
editor@2leafpress.org
www.2leafpress.org

2LEAF PRESS
is an imprint of the
Intercultural Alliance of Artists & Scholars, Inc. (IAAS),
a NY-based nonprofit 501(c)(3) organization that promotes
multicultural literature and literacy.
www.theiaas.org

Cover art: Jean-Michel Basquiat,
Boy and Dog in a Johnnypump, 1982,
acrylic, oil paintstick, and spray paint on canvas, 94½ x 165½
© The Estate of Jean-Michel Basquiat / ADAGP, Paris / ARS, New York 2013

Cover design: Miriam Ahmed
Book layout: Gabrielle David
Author photo: Richard "Vagabond" Beaumont

Library of Congress Control Number: 2013933165
ISBN-13: 978-0-9884-763-5-6 (Paperback)
ISBN-10: 978-0-9884-763-9-4 (eBook)

10   9   8   7   6   5   4   3   2   1

Published in the United States of America

First Edition | First Printing

2LEAF PRESS trade distribution is handled by University of Chicago Press / Chicago Distribution Center (www.press.uchicago.edu) 773.702.7010. Titles are also available for corporate, premium, and special sales. Please direct inquiries to the UCP Sales Department, 773.702.7248.

For Lynette Velasco,
Jan Carew,
Jayne Cortez,
Marlene Lillian Hawthrone-Thomas,
Yvonne E. Aiken, and
My uncle Denny "Cholo" Ortiz Bahamundi —

Ancestral

BROKE NOTE

BROKE BAROQUE is a nonlinear verse narrative in the voice of a homeless everyman named Broke, expounding on his existence and life experiences through conversational poems, tall tales, anecdotes, episodes, rants and jokes, much like that of Langston Hughes' Simple. Broke is also in the tradition of Charlie Chaplin's Tramp, as well as Nicanor Parra's Christ of Elqui, Zbigniew Herbert's Mr. Cogito and Richard Pryor's Mudbone, where these everyman personas critique modern society through satire, humor, irony and pathos.

POET LAUREATE OF THE BROKE

RONALD REAGAN'S HEAVILY MADE UP FACE and pompadour were used for two terms by multinationals and the far right to flood the ghettos with crack, destroy the black power movement—his assignment from his patron J. Edgar Hoover—and to drive the poor out of their homes and into the streets. He did this by ending housing subsidies and breaking the unions. The homeless began to appear shortly before his inauguration, an observation made in my Reagan era novel, *The Terrible Twos.* In his "Reagan's Legacy: Homelessness in America," Peter Dreier wrote:

> The most dramatic cut in domestic spending during the Reagan years was for low-income housing subsidies. Reagan appointed a housing task force dominated by politically connected developers, landlords and bankers. In 1982 the task force released a report that called for 'free and deregulated markets as an alternative to government assistance—advice Reagan followed. In his first year in office Reagan halved the budget for public housing and Section 8 to about $17.5 billion. And for the next few years he sought to eliminate federal housing assistance to the poor altogether.

> In the 1980s the proportion of the eligible poor who received federal housing subsidies declined. In 1970 there were 300,000 more low-cost rental units (6.5 million) than low-income renter households (6.2 million). By 1985 the number of low-cost units had fallen to 5.6 mil-

lion, and the number of low-income renter households had grown to 8.9 million, a disparity of 3.3 million units.

Another of Reagan's enduring legacies is the steep increase in the number of homeless people, which by the late 1980s had swollen to 600,000 on any given night—and 1.2 million over the course of a year."(1)

He started out in Hollywood and fulfilled the aims of his backers who in turn made him and his family rich. They needed some who would go where you wanted him to go, read a script and attach a smile to it. He came to office complaining about "black bucks" living on welfare and "welfare queens." In a sense, he was one of the first post-racers, blaming the poor for their situation.

Behind these moves lurked the Nazi policy of Dr. Raymond B. Cattell's Genthanasia, (2) the nonviolent means by which undesirable groups are eliminated. The media, which, during American history, has called for the extermination of blacks and Indians, played along by backing the book that claimed the sub-humanity of black people. *The Bell Curve*, by Charles Murray, which was financed by the Pioneer Fund, (3) a think-tank whose founders were pro-Nazi, received praise from the Jim Crow media and framed government policy. He was also the adviser for the insidious Wisconsin welfare program.

Some black members of the "Talented Tenth" (a group of intellectual elite African Americans) were used to say that the problems of a "black underclass" were traceable to their personal behavior. For their support of the Neo Con talking points, their careers were advancerd just as Nathan Glazer and Daniel Moynihan were rewarded with "whiteness" by blasting the poor.

Just as the secret government used a minority cultural contingent to undermine the art of protest, those same institutions worked with fallen intellectuals on the payroll of think tanks to clip the safety net.

Once in awhile they'd slip and reveal their plans for the poor. In the 1990s, Mayor Giuliani, who, under the instructions of the Manhattan Institute, which dabbles in Eugenics and whose chief spokesperson is *Daily News* columnist John McWhorter, set out to end rent control in New York. He unleashed the police on blacks and Hispanics in New York City and said in an unguarded moment that he would like to rid New York of the poor. The mayor probably learned his mean racist vindictiveness from his thug father who was arrested for assault and shared a cell with Harlem gangster, Bumpy Johnson.

Mayor Bloomberg, whose ancestors were stopped and frisked in Amsterdam, Warsaw, Paris and Berlin, is attempting to finish off the poor and homeless in New York by using the same Gestapo tactics that tormented his ancestors. Charles Blow of the *Times* says that police tactics are driving poor people out of the city so that Times Square, a neighborhood that once had character, looks like a Disney theme park. On 7th Avenue, you can have your picture taken with Mickey Mouse.

While there have been attempts in the past to elevate the needs of the poor as the primary concern of writers like John Reed, Richard Wright, Gwendolyn Brooks, Walter Lowenfels, Langston Hughes, Tillie Olson and others, this all changed with the arrival of the white middle class feminist and LGBT movements, who wouldn't be where they are without the sacrifices—indeed head whippings—that poor black and Puerto Rican drag queens took during battles with the police in San Francisco and New York. bell hooks, who is in literary exile as a result of her critique of a movement that puts racism in the background, says that white feminists, whose power has been endorsed by corporate America like Sprint, AT&T, J. P. Morgan, etcetera, told her that in order to succeed as a writer she had to write for them. This has meant, since the 1970s, a literature that demonizes not the one percent who control most of the country's resources but minority men. It was left to some rappers and Hip Hoppers to continue the storytelling set by the blues, and by the great African American poets and novelists. Unfortunately, many of them are not as successful on the page. That's where poets like Tony Medina come in.

Tony Medina's book is important because it picks up where we left off before minority literary culture was smothered by chick lit, hi and low, and gangsta fiction, written by people who serve up stereotypes to customers who can't get enough of this trash. His is a literature that does not blame the poor for their problems but places the blame where it belongs, the white patriarchal elite and its minority subdivision in culture and politics. This is not to say that black and Puerto Rican men can't be cruel to women, but because the white middle class feminist and LGBT movements are dependent upon being subsidized by the white patriarchal elite, they've scapegoated men who have little power, thereby distracting attention from the abuses of people who sell toxic mortgages and toxic food. How many poets today have the moxie to take on Monsanto as Medina does? How many are even aware of the gene spliced evil products with which big Agri are flooding our supermarkets?

As a result, those who are downtrodden, those who are looked upon with contempt, "stabbed with eyes," have few advocates. This is where the poet comes in. The poets are left with the task that journalists used to have. To comfort the afflicted and afflict the comfortable.

Medina's people drink beer and not champagne, the bags are not made by Vuitton, the bags are body bags. Medina tells us how the broke get by, how they live, their day to day quest for survival, the contempt by which people hold them. This is an ugly world of shit and vomit, of drugs and alcohol where broke husbands abandon broke wives, where people live in refrigerators in cardboard dwellings, where pigeons and dogs get more food than they. Rats and roaches rule. Healthcare always ends in extractions. Where being jailed or hospitalized is a vacation for the broke. These are places where you can get a few meals every day.

Medina barters with his readers like those guys who haunt the bars and restaurants with a whole store tucked away in their overcoats. If you don't want a watch, hey, they'll sell you sunglasses. Medina's versatility allows the reader to choose what they want. A villanelle is taken from the royal court and put on the block. Dazzling puns like:

"I begs your Bacardon."

Medina is not a tourist who is out to sell the unsuspecting a fake take on the ghetto from a middle class region like the white girl who wrote a ghetto memoir which turned out to be fake, yet praised by *Times* book critic, Michiko Kakutani, a feminist who practices her feminism on the brothers, yet does a critical lap dance for big league misogynists like Saul Bellow. (The writer got a $100,000 advance). He knows about crackheads. He knows that it is a crime to be poor. It is a crime to be poor not only according to the usual Genthanasiers but by the black and Hispanic cultural and intellectual elite who make money putting down 35-year-old grandmothers living in the projects. Poet laureates are chosen from this group, or those who are so weak, so obtuse, and so unintelligible that they get invited to Bush's or Obama's White House Literary Festivals.

You don't need no dictionary to know where Medina stands.

Since he moons the establishment like one of his characters moons a priest, Medina will never be poet laureate. As long as over fifty-year-old white men make the selections, Tony Medina will never be U.S. Poet Laureate. He is the Poet Laureate of the Broke. Like Jean-Michel Basquiat who takes Hip Hop to another level, Medina covers some of the same territory as Hip Hop's best. Tupac. Public Enemy. Dead Prez.

Let's hope that Medina's book is a renewal. A turning point. A departure from the past thirty years of literary decadence during which privileged whites and their black auxiliary complained about their double oppression while the truly oppressed were being flushed down the toilet.

Francis E.W. Harper (1825-1911) wrote about black women being auctioned off by the southern 1% who owned slaves and made the white poor fight a war for them. Today's "doubly oppressed" academics and media celebrities spend hours on TV discussing their hair. ❖

— Ishmael Reed
Oakland, California
March 2013

WORKS CITED

(1) Peter Drier, "Reagan's Legacy Homelessness in America," the National Housing Institute (NHI), Issue #135, May/June 2004, retrieved from http://www.nhi.org/online/issues/135/reagan.html

(2) Genthanasia is simply an obfuscation of genocide. What Cattell calls genthanasia, Van den Bergh calls "ethnocide and genocide committed by elites."

(3) Started in 1937 by textile magnate Wickliffe Draper, the Pioneer Fund's original mandate was to pursue "race betterment" by promoting the genetic stock of those "deemed to be descended predominantly from white persons who settled in the original thirteen states prior to the adoption of the Constitution." Today, it still funds studies of race and intelligence, as well as eugenics, the "science" of breeding superior human beings that was discredited by various Nazi atrocities. The Pioneer Fund has supported many of the leading Anglo-American race scientists of the last several decades as well as anti-immigration groups such as the Federation for American Immigration Reform (FAIR)." Southern Poverty Law Center.

"Somebody is always trying to take disadvantage of me."

— Jesse B. Semple

BROKE BAROQUE

I was a lucky stiff
Stuffed in a garbage bag
    With a Day-Glo toe tag
The size of a Winnebago
    Parallel parked against
A callus so thick and red
    You'd swear it was a blow hard
Right-wing televangelist
    Screaming holy Jesus hell or high water
About the end of the world
    And the second coming
Of Burl Ives on 5th Ave & 34th St
    Oblong objects have always been
My Achilles' heel
    It's no wonder I heard
A squeal
    When the orderly
Tried to put me in
    The freezer but couldn't
Get past my ankle
    That got rankled
In the coroner's report
    He said I was left
For dead
    In the slums of Calcutta
In the favelas of Rio de Janero
    In the tombs of Timbuktu
In the wounds of South Bronx fumes
    And Biloxi blues
On a nowhere man cruise
    My head was a cardboard box
My liver an anthill of the Savannah
    Manna from heaven so hard
Nearly knocked me upside down
    But I survived with
My wits about me
    A roguish lout going
Toe-to-toe with the best of 'em

From the ass-end of a bottle
Of cheap perfume
    Drunk off the flames
Of fruit of the looms
    Where to my surprise
I surmise
    The cries of wine resides
In a dark alley
    In broad daylight
Tapping the bottle for residue
    This is how my pulse
Was taken
    In exchange for
Bacon
    They say the poor would make
Prime choice ribs
    Tell that to Eve
When you see her

BROKE BAIL OUT

You may have been the first
In a hearse
But let me tell you

About my purse
And how the lint
Is so lonely

It cries
Every time
The wind blows

Through it
You may be without
A rib

But let me tell you
About this here cage
And how I rattle

A tin cup
Against it yelling
Filthy screws Filthy screws

As a form of entertainment
Just to get a few coins
Tossed my way

BROKE VILLANELLE

Isn't it enough you charge for flies in soup
Monopolize water and air and even despair
Such flames of hell withstood from a pigeon coop

In order for us lowly meek to loom and brood
About our place in this pecking order new world odor
Isn't it enough you charge for flies in soup

Cold mathematics understood by a flame retardant tool
You eat and breathe and drink clean water as we smolder
Such flames of hell withstood from a pigeon coop

Land gobbled up like entrees of rich Monsanto food
What falls from the table is what we lizard lap
Isn't it enough you charge for flies in soup

What's mine is yours is surely understood by fools
Divine Right and Imminent Domain we lack like shoes
Such flames of hell withstood from a pigeon coop

Should we call in sick the rest of our dazed tased days
Bequeath you flesh and bones and ill-gotten veins
Isn't it enough you charge for flies in soup
Such flames of hell withstood from a pigeon coop

BROKE CAT GAUCHO TONGUE

I'm a ghetto gaucho
A homeless housing project honcho
In a recycled dingy white plastic trash bag poncho

I ride on a New York City rat
With a big garbage can lid sombrero hat
And a gold tooth badge

I lasso tumbleweed weaves
Rollin' up on me in the middle of the street
Makin' me think it's some dog shit come to life

To pistol whip me
I shoot buckshot naps and pillow blanket
Comforter lint peas

Off the back of your neck
With the ease of a sneeze
Or windmill breeze

I'm a ghetto gaucho
A neo-nuyo sheriff
Of rodentary Five-O drive-bys

Slithering about
Bumping my belly
On slime

I dine on swine
And swindle my way
Past dope slinging hags

In drag
Dressed in Donna Karan
Original see-through

Shower curtains
And alligator shoes
With roaches and pigeons

And pissy drunk wino
Alley cats in their teeth
Whining beneath windows

Of politicians pissing from
Pulpits into mouths
Of potential voters whose

Ballot box is an outhouse
Or W.C. in the fields
Of plantation dreams come to life

In Technicolor on TV and the big screen
I scream on those who scream
I 'tis of thee

America what you why you
Mean to me
I ain't done shit

But try and feed
My chil'ren
I'm a ghetto gaucho

Brandishing a broke baton
And a six-pack of water guns
Kickin' ass juiced on bottles

Of Puerto Rican rum for fun
I begs your Bacardon
I'm a bounty hunter for hirin'

I gets off on firing
Into a crowd of constipated consumers
Who I assumers complained about

A slight rise in taxes
They asses I waxes
With axes to grind

Stuffing them with formaldehyde
Placing them in the
Museum of Natural Hysterectomies

I'm a ghetto gaucho
Paid to place you under arrest
As you rest beneath my flat feet shoes

Gasping for air
Clutching your chest
Watching your sockets pop eye blood

I'm a ghetto gaucho
Occupying territory
Like a flood

Flushing you out to the outskirts
Of democracy and reform into
The norm of corporate American rebates

Privatized prison fees
Non-voluntary up with your hands
Down on your knees

As I confiscate more lands
Coercing crumbs from the mouths
Of sleeping beggars and bums

I'm a ghetto gaucho
I catch criminals like frogs catch flies
I raise blood pressures

With lies
Convict mud suckers
Who wanna get high

I Saran Wrap pedestrians
With body bags
Indifferent splinters of blackjack spit

As I ticket them for jaywalking
With their house slippers stuck in shit
I videotape me beatin' civilization

Into uncivilized civilian ass
With the butt of my chokehold jokes
Show it at the Policeman's Ball

Where we have a ball
Watching it like a bachelor party
Porno show with *Oh Danny Boy* bagpipes
Background music flow in tow

I'm a ghetto gaucho
A new millennium
Diet plan

I can make you lose weight
By laying you down
Six feet
Underground

BROKE CONFESSION

If I was worth
My weight
In gold
I'd still
Be broke

If I had
A dime
For every time
I got rejected
Or for every
Seemingly sincere
Sorry, I'm broke
I'd be
Rich

If I
Relied on
Such wishful
Thinking
Or on
Handouts to
Survive
I'd die
Of starvation

The only reason
I'm still here
Is from eating
Cardboard boxes
And drinking
Rainwater

BROKE ON THE JOB

Sometimes I put in a twenty-four hour day
I work so hard I miss breakfast I miss lunch
I miss dinner and all the cobwebs in between
    By the time I'm finished—I'm finished
    My feet hurt for being on them
    All day, my back bent and spent
Scrounging through angry
Trash bags for broke bottles
And cans bent on rolling away
    On shoestring of old wino back alley pissed
Off wind having me dive headfirst into
Slime and scorch of sewers where rats sin, drink gin
And play timbales with the tin I'm chasin'
    Wrestled from forked teeth grins
    Hissing at me with ratty tail whips
To the chin—but I grin—and bear it
And in the end—win—tossing it in my bag
Hauling it off like a back-breaking bail of hay
    What seems like twelve hours
    Takes all day, work so hard for no
    Breakfast lunch or dinner
By the time I'm finished—I'm famished
My feet hurt for being on them
All day, back bent and spent
    Get so tired and hungry
    I don't know whether I'm walking
    Or stumbling passing gas like glass
Stomach volcanic with pain
I could barely sleep
On this bed of concrete

BROKE BOP SHUFFLE

Don't stab me in the doorway
   With those eyes of yours

Don't curse me under your breath
   Sucking your teeth and balling up

Your face like a fist wishing I was dead
   Or that I would disappear — or both

Because I'm ugly and dirty and haven't
   Washed my clothes in I don't know

How many years or because
   I move too slow getting off

The train while you get on
   I can't help it if my feet

Are swelled up elephantine
   Gangrenous track-marked

Open sores red and raw
   Sliced open grapefruits

The next time I'd wrap them in
   Plastic bags so I won't

Offend you or upset your
   Stomach

But I can't help it if I don't
   Have shoes

BROKE IN JAIL

Can you believe this place?
    A rally for the only political prisoner
On Death Row, Mumia Abu-Jamal,

    A journalist from Philly framed
For killing some cop,
    Just happened to take place where I live

Which of course is on the street
    And I get swept up in the agitated aftermath
By Five-O and hauled off to jail

    First they tried to say I was
Part of the demonstration
    And I resisted arrest

I know my lips were moving
    But I wasn't Protesting
Hell, you go without food

    As long as I have and you'd be
Gumming air too!
    Then they said since I didn't

Have five dollars they were gonna
    Have to arrest me for vagrancy
Ain't that a bitch

    Here I am on the streets
'Cause the law makes it legal
    To starve me

Only to find out
    It's against the law
To be broke!

BROKE WET DREAMS

Living on the streets
Ages you before your time

Body odor alone
Backfires on you

Adding wrinkles to
Hang your hunger pains on

Even old people bump into me
And say—*Hey, Pop!*

Which really doesn't bother
Me much because I look forward

To such signs of affection
It's comforting to be

Acknowledged
Especially these days

When I'm at my lowest
And loneliest

Why just the other day
Most of my friends drowned

When a water main burst
Flooding the subway

The tracks just filled up
And flushed them out

The station like headless rats
Rolling around a cesspool

Of shit and vomit
I was fortunate enough to

Wake from my coma and barely
Escaped with just a slight fracture

And as wrinkled as a wet prune
It wasn't as big a tragedy as the

Inconvenience it cost commuters
Trying to get home from work

Besides, the media made light of it
By allowing the mayor a photo-op

Where he said at a City Hall news conference
They had no business being there—

Can't they read? The law clearly states
That the homeless are forbidden to

Panhandle and should abstain from sleeping
In the subway or face felony

Charges and possible prosecution.
Anyway, consider it spring cleaning—

At least the tourists can't say we're not
Cleaning our subways.

BROKE PICK-OF-THE-DAY

I believe that old saying
That God works
In mysterious ways

And the Forest Gump
Revised version
About life being

Like a box of chocolates
You never know what
You're going to get

And usually
In my situation
You never get

But there are exceptions
Why just the other day
A man who went berserk

Stabbing everyone
In his entire family
With a Ginsu knife

Carjacked a woman's car
At knifepoint
And went on a psychotic rampage

As cops chased him down
Crowded downtown streets
The car came rambling down

The street mowing down
A line of homeless people
Laid out along the curb

I was at the end
Of this already broken line
Of broken down men

Who cushioned me
From the steel jaws
Of the grill of the car

And the bloody nose
Of its front license plate
Receiving minimal damage

Up until this time
It had never dawned on me
That my misfortune was a result

Of another man's fortune
But now the tables were turned
And I took advantage

Of the situation
It's not every day
That I get so lucky

As to fake being broken
Ending up in a nice
Warm hospital bed

Eating three meals a day
Pampered by nurses
If only I had five bucks

To turn the TV on
To see if I made
The Six O'clock News

Or find out
What lottery number
Came out

BROKE DICK DOG

As a child I always envied pigeons
Their ability to spring and fly

At a moment's notice
From place to place

That's why I would chase them frantically
Through parks, driving my mother

Crazy with paranoia at the fear that I would
Fall and bang my head or scrape my knee

Nowadays, I envy the little bastards even more
They always have food to eat

People don't hesitate to give them handouts
What makes it worse is that these damn birds

Are always in my face shaking their little
Arrogant booties bragging about

The breadcrumbs they spend the greater
Part of the day plucking from the ground

And shitting on my face while I'm asleep
Letting me know how lazy I am

And that the early bird catches the worm
It's gotten to the point where when I chase them

They don't fly away anymore
They just stay there staring me down

Like a New York City rat
So when prospective donors come by

I'm usually caught in an embarrassing
Compromising position

On my hands and knees
Like a broke dick dog going nose-to-nose

With a pigeon for a piece of discarded bread
As hard as the dentures of the

Old lady who hurls it from a park bench
Pitying me my scraped knees

BROKE BACK PAYMENTS

It's not that I'm bored
Or that I enjoy

Being a bully
Or that I have aspirations

Of joining a circus
That I sit back

On my elbows
On the grass

In this park
Juggling squirrels

With my feet
But that they

Were a few nuts short
On their acorn payments

BROKE BELIEVER

When I was a heavy boozer
And my wife kicked me out
Of our cardboard box
I never believed in Santa Claus

But she did and always claimed to see
The fat fuck clinking around outside
On Christmas Eve—*But what did he*
Bring us? I would always yell

This! she would scream
Producing one of my pint bottles
From underneath her dress and
Between her legs, hurling it at me

Until finally after one lump too many
I got the message and went on my own
Trudging through the snow
It wasn't until the cold hit me

Splitting through my bones
And hunger pains started playing
The xylophone across my ribs
Making me high with anguish

That I had my first revelation
I heard the clinking of empty beer bottles
Strung up and dragging along the backend
Of a cardboard sled by telephone wire

Coming out of total darkness in an alley
Then out of nowhere
Sitting on the cardboard sled
A fat white wino with a red nose

And red cheeks was yelling—
Onward Prancer! Onward Dancer!
Onward Donner! & Blitzen & Sonny Boner!
To a team of alley cats furiously chasing rats

Pulling the sled across a thin sheet of ice and snow
On a row of garbage dumpsters
And the old wino yelled down to me—
Hey! Rudolph! Merry fuckin' Christmas!

And flung a half-empty bottle of cheap wine at me
Hitting me on the head like hocking at a spittoon
Riding off into the pitch-black sky
Toward a jaundiced moon

BROKE BROKEN

Subway car seats
Can be quite torturous

When someone sits
On your face

In a crowded
Train

I wake up
Like this

Sometimes
During early

Morning
Rush hours

If I wanted
A nose job

I would've
Kept my day job

Instead it seems
Even when

I try my hardest
Not to kiss

Ass that's just
What I

End up
Doing

BROKE WITHOUT HEAD & SHOULDERS

Those of us
   Who are forced
To sleep
   Outdoors

And can't
   Afford to
Comb
   And wash

And cut
   Our hair
Must be
   Very careful

That while
   We are
Sleeping
   A family

Of five
   Doesn't
Move
   Into it

It'll be
   A bitch
Trying to
   Evict them

Like dumping
   Somebody
After you've
   Been dumped

BROKE WITH INDIGESTION

Because I always
Had trouble

With science
In school

And frequently
Cut class

And flunked
I did not know

What a total
Eclipse

Of the sun
Was

So when
I woke up

One day
I thought

I was having a
Bad dream or a

Heart attack or stroke
Or that I was dead

Or had had a flashback
Of the time

Con Edison
Turned the electricity off

In my eyes
Imagine that

To think I was
Gonna give up

Eating out
Of garbage cans

BROKE WITH HEADACHE

After I spent years
Banging my head
Against trees

Trying to
Detonate the
Bugging devices

The State
Put in my hair
I finally gave in

And went with
The flow
I dreaded

My hair
Now I walk around
Peeking through

First floor windows
Twirling my locks
At television sets

Trying to
Pick up
HBO

BROKE GOOD WILL

They say charity
Begins at home
But what if
You have no home

Don't get me wrong
I believe in charity
Hell, I'll be the
Last one to

Ever turn down a
Handout or two
That's why
When a friend

Of mine
Tried donating
Parts of his body
To science

But was rejected
Because of years
Of poor health
From living

On the street
I took them
Trading him
For a used coat

Someone gave me
The act of giving
Made me feel
So good

I even took up
A collection
To replace
His body parts

BROKE ON GLASS

I know
That there
Are times
When I
Can be a
Pest and
Be as annoying
As a fruit fly
Buzzing
In your ear

But all I'm
Trying to do
Is make
An extra dollar
Cleaning your
Windshield of
All the bird shit
Dirt dust
Car exhaust
And gnats

You don't
Have to
Treat me
Like one
And put the
Pedal
To the metal
As soon as the
Light
Turns green!

Fuck the fact
That you broke
My squeegee
How am I
Gonna get
Back home
And who's gonna
Peel my ass
Off this
Windshield

BROKE BATH

If you think
Living outdoors
Can be hazardous
To your health
Try doing what I do
To make a living

Working outdoors
Can be just as brutal
Try cleaning
Car windshields
During rush hour
To and from work

Sometimes people
Don't want to be
Bothered   they
Peel off as soon
As you come
Up to the car

And if you're not fast
On your feet you'll
End up cleaning a windshield
Not with a squeegee
But with your face
Tongue teeth and gums

And even though I may have lost
My kneecaps
In the grill of a car
Pulling off on its way to a
Real car wash and
Blood from my face

Covers the windshield
Like a sun visor or a
Thin sheet of tarpaulin
I can't complain – hell
I got a free lift
And a shampoo and shower

BROKE BURNT-OUT BUILDINGS

Sometimes I think
There's a conspiracy
Against me

I don't mean
The fact
That everytime

I try
To cop
A squat

In one of those
Burnt-out
Abandoned buildings

The city holds on to
And refuses to turn over
To those of us

Who have no homes
The ones that are
Always collapsing

While I'm sleeping
As if the floors
Were made of cardboard

I'd accept the blame
For taking such a risk
But when the mayor

Goes around
Hiring demolition teams
To dynamite and bulldoze

Abandoned buildings
Whose floors don't collapse
On their own

While I'm inside sleeping
Then I begin to worry
It's not that

I'm paranoid
Or delusional
But when I

Can't even find
A decent place
To sleep

Be it
A park bench or
A subway car seat

Or a street grater
Without some teenager
Setting my clothes

On fire
Then I begin
To worry

And think
That maybe
They're on the take

If cops can
Pay crackheads to
Set up wars

Between drug dealers
And rival gangs
They surely

Can afford to
Take me out to
Meet their quotas

And make the mayor happy
That the city's getting cleaned up
In time for tourist season

Besides it's better
To torch me or
Blow me up

Rather than to risk
Having to touch me
As they kick me out

Of parks and subways
Not to mention that they
Save the city a fortune on

Surgical gloves

BROKE CITIZEN'S ARREST

A serial groper who
Approached women

From behind, then
Fondled them was arrested

After getting his cuff links
Caught in the strap of a

Cross Your Heart Bra

BROKE MOTTO

When it's free
I don't complain

When it costs
An arm and a leg

I raise Cain!

BROKE WITH BULB

It wouldn't take
Intense cross-examination

To get me to confess
To losing a couple of toes

To frostbite
But I lucked out

I took advantage
Of the situation

In order to survive
Another day

Without food
I boiled them

In a tin can
And made a hearty soup

I was going to share
With an old friend

Who was not up to
Searching for his own food

But unfortunately
He too could not

Brave the cold
And I watched

His lungs collapse
His eyes staring at me

From a blue wrinkled face
While my toe stuck out his mouth

Like a red Christmas bulb

BROKE FOUND POEM

Police say
A motorcyclist

Dead set against
Wearing a helmet

Participating in a
Protest ride

Against helmet laws
In upstate New York

Died after he flipped
Over the handlebars

And hit his head
On the pavement

BROKE "THIS JUST IN"

Homeless man
    Chases down

Dog at
    Gramercy Park

For his
    Sweater

And gets
    Impounded by

Dogcatchers

BROKE LITIGATION

I want
To sue
The media
And the IRS
For defecation
Of character

BROKE AT THE ASPCA

If only this net was
Lined with feathers

Or cotton or plaid strips
Of flannel

Then maybe I'll give
Up the dog's

Sweater
So the catcher'll

Release me
But fuck it

I'm freezing
They have fur and fat

And sleep and eat
Better than me

Besides
The kennel will be

Better than
Someone's doorstep

Only what will
I do when my time

Is up and no one wants
To take me home

What will I do when they
Come to put me

To sleep

BROKE AWAKENING

Mornings I wake
To look at life
Through concertina
Razor wire
Eyes

Closed shut by frozen
Tears and puss
My bones welded
Into the bench

Or a rough
Concrete slab
Of earth
Making ice patches
On my back

My neck stiff
As a brick

If I try to rise
Like this
I'll crumble
And collapse

Into a pile
Of ashes

BROKE REFLECTION

When I was a child
And lived on Simpson Street
In the South Bronx
We used to camp out
In front of our building
Roasting hot dogs
And marshmallows
In a garbage can fire
Because we were too poor
To go camping

Now as a grown man
I'm still broke
But I have the good fortune
To relive my youth
Only this time
I'm the hot dog

And marshmallow

BROKE POLITICS

I don't harbor
Feelings
Of resentment
Towards those
Able to sleep
With impunity

On a soft bed
Even though
I wake up
With concertina
Razor wire
Glued to my eyelids

I understand the extent
And weight
Of the law
It's just
That I'm losing
So much weight

I wouldn't want
To cheat the State
Of its terror tactics
By undermining it
With an unmotivated
Hunger strike

I know it's a crime
To be poor but
I wouldn't want to
Be accused
Of being a
Subversive

BROKE LOGIC

All I have are these cans
I drag in this plastic
Garbage bag

Which also serves
As a tent or sleeping bag
When it's cold and raining

To some my lack
Of clarity may seem
Like a lie or insanity

Actually
All I have
Are these cans
I drag

A plastic
Garbage bag
A tent
And a sleeping bag

I have more things
Now than when
I started
This poem!

BROKE IN BELLEVUE

Sometimes when it's cold out
And I can't go into the
Subways to sleep and
Keep warm

Or end up getting
Kicked out
By cops
Who won't even

Take me into
A nice warm cell
For breaking the law
Or if I feel cocky

And stubborn
And kick off the
Policeman's Ball
In the staircase

By coming back
And forth
Until the officer's
Too tired to

Tango with me
Or his shift is over
And when the shelters
Are overcrowded

And too dangerous
To sleep with both eyes shut
I run around the street
Like a mad baboon

Gone ape shit
So the paramedics
Can come and get me
Fitted for a white jacket

Never mind the cell
With the rubber walls
The electric shock treatment
Is what keeps me warm

BROKE REGRETS

You know
You haven't

Made much
Of your life

When you live
On a park bench

And the newspaper
You use

To keep
Yourself warm

Has your obituary

BROKE SUCCESS

I remember
When I used to
Eat sardines
For dinner

Then I blew up
And couldn't get
The limo through
The McDonald's drive-thru

Now I eat
Mayonnaise
And hand
Sandwiches

BROKE CHOICE

I must confess
In my situation
There's not much you
Could do to get by

I mean
Collecting bottles
And cans or
Selling used books
Is not like
Selling drugs
Where you can
Rake in the
Big bucks

But I'm not
Messing with drugs
They're bad news
For you and the poor bastard
Who thinks he needs them
Who wants that
On their head

I mean don't get me
Wrong
With books you
Can also get high
Off your supply
And not make any
Money
They'd kill you
Sure as drugs would

But even though
I may die of starvation
At least I'll be able to
Read my obituary

BROKE DATE

Bachelorette number one
If I were to take

You out
For dinner

And a movie
But could only

Afford to
Run you down town

Along Central Park West
Into midtown

And stand with you
In front of a restaurant window

Staring at other people's food
And drink

Because I don't have the money
To really wine and dine you

And after your eyes
Fill up on filet mignon and *vino*

I'd stroll you over
To a window display at Macy's

Radio Shack The Wiz or Crazy Eddie's
To check out what's on the tube

Would you say
I tried my best

To romance you
Wouldn't you think

I loved you

BROKE PUSHED

Electric cattle prods
Move us along swiftly

Out of the subway station
Off of benches out of parks

So old women can sit
And children can play

Without having to face
What may be in store

For them on their way
In or on their way out

BROKE BFFS

Some of my best friends are white
They're always thinking of me

Why just the other night
They got drunk on Tequila

And started thinking about
A tree they'd like to decorate

With my body

BROKE IMAGINING

Just imagine if you had
To pay in installments
For glimpses of the sun

And on hot nights
You had to pay a tariff
For cool strips of wind like gingham

Paying for a slight breeze
May mean having to give up
Your portion of sun

Or that the water
That flows freely
Through fire hydrants

Had to have a
Down payment
Before you could

Soak your head
Dip your feet
Off the curb or

Stretch out your tongue
Hell, it's not too farfetched
I mean life is so expensive

In this town
And you pay for
Everything else

How much will it cost to
Fill your lungs with
Clean air

BROKE TIMES

I used to get gigs from people with cars
    Who had the luxury of coming and going
        By choice instead of by force or by chance

Of course I didn't validate park
    Or carjack or steal hubcaps
        Windshield wipers and mirrors

I mean strangely enough they didn't
    Have me cleaning their car or using a squeegee
        Or even guarding it from vandals

Or people tired and lazy enough to
    Lean on the door sit on the hood
        And trip the car alarm

I used to paint and put up signs that read
    No Radio Inside or *No Valubles No Car Alarm Inside*
        As if the car alarm were not valuable enough!

Nowadays with the economy
    The way it is they have me
        Write and post signs that say

Please steal this piece of shit car
    From me so I can collect
        Insurance on it

TONY MEDINA

63

BROKE FEAR

Being evicted from your home
Is not nearly as scary
As being evicted
From no home

It's scary sleeping
Out in the open
Never knowing
If someone will slit

Your throat
Set you on fire
Molest you
Rob you

Kick you
Beat you
Have you
Carried off

By ants and
Dumped in
The sewer like
Bad fish

BROKE ROUTINE

A landscape of roaches
Laying on their backs
    Blood splashed
    Onto the streets
To wash off
The cracks
    Opening a soda bottle
    For a brother
Who said his hands
Were too greasy
    Because he was
    Eating chitterlings
Standing on bread lines
And soup kitchen lines
    Spilling out
    Onto the street
As if it were a
Crack house or
    Methadone clinic
    Pigeons lean off buildings
Waiting to shit and tease
And pluck bread
    From our hands
    Fights will break out
The police will side
With the pigeons
    Giving out tickets
    Roaches do back strokes
On hot shitty streets
Covered in feathers

BROKE IMPRESSION

I refuse to believe
That all cops are bad
Or smart and sinister
And sick and experimental
As Nazi scientists
Collecting human skin
For writing britches
Lampshades
And bars of soap

But I knew of one cop
Who *was* a motherfucker!
He walked his beat
Through parks
And was jealous
Of the homeless
Who lived and
Stretched out
Along the benches

He was fat
And spent his hours
Eating bagels and donuts
And being that
He wasn't allowed to
Sit his big ass down
While on his beat
He would frequently
Harass and harangue us

Once he sat on
Someone's chest
Yelling—
Okay!
You wanna be
A bench?
I'll make you
My bench!
Until his lungs exploded

BROKE REALIZATION

How can I complain
About not having a
Roof over my head

When the sky is
My ceiling
Most places are cramped

Ceilings are low
And make you feel
Boxed in

In my case
I have the sun
And moon and stars

Clouds spread out wide
And far
Who but I

Can boast
About being able to
House trees

When what most
People get are
Merely dried-out

Flowerpots
And dusty-ass
Rubber tree plants

BROKE HEAD ON HORSEBACK

I fall prey to delusions of grandeur
Sometimes I straddle splintered
Park benches and fancy myself

Quixote on the broke back
Of Rocinante stabbing at windmills
But I'm not like Don Quixote

I haven't read much
I grew up watching TV
Hollywood breastfed me

All I ever learned of chivalry
I learned from people like
Errol Flynn and John Wayne

It wasn't until I lived my life
On the streets
And was constantly harassed by cops

That I realized that John Wayne
Was really the bad guy
And not the Indians

It took several cops to help me come
To this conclusion
When they beat me off

The carousel at Central Park with
Flashlights as I tried to ride
My horse backwards

Into town like I was the
New sheriff out to make
Things right

BROKE BACK ALLEY SCRAPS

I wonder if in restaurants
They charge extra for
E. coli bacteria found in your
Hamburger or your beef stew

It seems that someone like me
Doesn't have to worry about this
Seeing that I don't eat much
Let alone eat out

But come to think of it
I do eat out—
Of garbage cans!
I hang around back alleys

Poking through trash cans
At the leftovers diners and
Fast food restaurants
Throw away

This is a strange and risky sport
Which requires cunning and logic
And sometimes a lot of rolls
Of toilet paper

At times the E. coli can grow so huge
They'd wrestle you into dark shadows
Putting a plastic knife to your throat
Threatening to take your money or your life

For someone like me who already
Has a weak stomach and bad heart
I don't need the added stress
So I end up giving them everything I have

Which is nothing but my will
To fight

TONY MEDINA

69

BROKE BAPTISM

I know I'm no Job
I can't boast of ever
Having any kind of fortune
Let a lone a reversal of fortune

It's true that Job lost his property
And his children
But for what it's worth
I have been removed

From my place of residence
And I have on occasion
Lost control
Of my bowels

You may sit in judgment
And say that it was my fault
That I shouldn't have been
Drinking or eating out of garbage cans

And I accept full responsibility
For any personal wrong doing
I agree with policies of repentance
But to have me walk around the streets

With soiled trousers on the hottest day
Of the summer without a decent change
Of underwear is really shitty
The least you could do

Is get me a pair of pants
From the Salvation Army
Put yourself in my shoes
For once

Besides giggling and making snide
Asides and remarks with your face
Squished up in disgust or surprise
The least you could do is turn on

A fire hydrant so I could
Wash my nasty ass and clothes
And not continue to assault your nose
You have enough problems

Dealing with the sun
Driving your blood pressure up
You don't need my shit
Cutting your lungs and giving you asthma

What am I suppose to do
Wait for a fire to break out to
Jump in front of the fireman's hose
To get a decent bath

And you would think that in my time
Of great despair that I would be able to
Count on God to clear the air –
But even He rejected me!

Following a maddening barrage
Of snickers and jeers
That trailed me from the street
Like flies

I ducked into the nearest
Church for Salvation
I tried to wash my soiled pants
But the priest would not allow me to

Enter into the church
As he instructed
His congregation to
Pray and chant at me:

Get ye behind me, Satan!
Get ye behind me, Satan!
Scaring the living shit
Out of me

When they rose up out of their pews
As if they were about to
Receive their wine and wafers
I gave them a piece of my Holy Communion

And mooned them
But before they could get to me
And I got through the door
I ended up dipping my ass in the

Holy water!

BROKE AMBIANCE

Sometimes I wish I had
Some kitchen curtains for
The refrigerator box I live in

Plastic bags do the trick
But ruin the mood
I'm trying to set

I always long for the
Comforts of home
Where I can stretch out

In a real bed
Safe and warm
Away from the

Glaring teeth of artificial light
Wrestling with the moon
And the chaos and debris

Of the streets
And not dream or pretend
That these strips

Of plastic bags
Are the same pattern
As the curtains used to make

My mother's last dress

TONY MEDINA 73

BROKE COMPETITION

I always pretend that the fountain
In front of the Metropolitan Museum of Art
Is the Fountain of Youth

The coins alone could erase years
Of Misery and despair
From my life

Coins that tourists toss off as readily
As a pair of shoes
On the side of the bed

At the end of the day
Instead of forking them over
To people like me

But I'm hip to their game
I know that everyone
Makes wishes

And dreams that they'll come true
That's why I take a straw
And breathe through it

As I lay under water
Catching coins with my
Hands feet and teeth

Who was to know
That there would be
Another poor slob

Like me
On the other side
With a stick

And a piece of gum
Jabbing me in my ribs
And eyes

BROKE TRAVEL BROCHURE

Living on the streets of New York
Is like being in somebody's guts

Where rats flip you
Like pizza

Juggling you
With their feet

While roaches applaud
The funk you bring

Carrying you
On their

Shoulders
Like a game-winning

Football team
Spiking you

On the shitty badge
Of a cop

Dragging you
By the neck

Or the ankle
And shoving

Your face
In your own

Vomit or shit
And piss

Evicting you
Into the sewer

Of your own despair
Like a headless fish

OD'ed on a teaspoon of water
Even bacteria would be afraid of

BROKE TALE LIGHTS

I don't take hallucinogens
But you wouldn't know that
From the last job I had

I used to be a rap artist
But I stuttered
Every time I tried to perform

I would break out into spastic
Displays of spraying spit
Until the entire first five rows

Were drowned and I was a
Puddle of wrinkled sweat
Twitching on the floor of the stage

With the rest of the audience
Booing me worse than
The Apollo

It got so bad
That I developed
Tourette's syndrome

And the only job I could get
Was hailing cabs for travelers
And tourists on 34th Street

At Penn Station
Or at local airports
I would lean off the curb

Stick out my arm and yell – *Taxi!*
But the memory of my last gig
Would plague me

And I would spazz out and jerk
Uncontrollably until I was
An endless series of facial tics and

Obscenities hurled at an invisible
Audience along with the word
Taxi! Taxi! until the entire street was a

Stockpile of yellow taxicabs stopping
And going stopping and going, skidding off
Into pile-ups and traffic jams

BROKE RELATION

My marriage
To a streetlight

Was dissolved by
Neighborhood punks

Who knocked
Its bulb out

With a rock
Being afraid

Of the dark
And the feelings

Of loneliness
It brings

I moved on
Panhandling

From place
To place

To buy batteries
For my flashlight

BROKE BUMMING CIGARETTES

I don't smoke
But for some reason

Instead
Of giving me coins

When I panhandle
People are always

Giving me cigarettes
I'm hip to what

The Surgeon General says
So I don't mess

With the stuff
But I'd wish

He'd say something
About poverty

Homelessness
And hunger

Them's hazardous
To your health too!

BROKE HIGHER EDUCATION

People always think
That since

I live on
The street

I must be
Uneducated

The truth is
I did graduate

From high school
And got my education

Shit
I learned

At an early age
That one

Take away one
Is zero!

I even
Went on

To college
I've been

Studying
Street life

And hunger
For so long

I got a
PhD in

Poverty

TONY MEDINA 81

BROKE LUCK

When it comes
To money

I have
The worst

Luck
In the

World
I've never

Been good
With it

Why just
The other day

At the shelter
I was playing

Monopoly
And wound up

On welfare

BROKE MARRIED WITHOUT CHILDREN

I never did become a father
Come to think of it I'm glad
I didn't have kids

I wouldn't want them
To see me like this
Without a place of my own

Without a space that they
Could call home
Never having heat or hot water

Not knowing when the next
Meal will come
Wearing somebody's

Hand-me-downs
Wrestling with roaches
And rats for crumbs

Besides I wouldn't
Want them to see me
Argue all the time

And fight with their mother
(My wife) who would've been
Such a bad influence

Who cussed like a sailor
And used phrases like
I gotta go take a dump!

Who smoked like a chimney
Who when I asked
Do you want children or

Do you want a pack of Marlboros?
Chose the latter and went out
For one and never came back

TONY MEDINA

83

BROKE JUSTICE

Taking the law into my own hands
I threw my first wife out of the

Window of our cardboard house
Because while she sat on the tin can

Chock full o'Nuts commode
She took a bowl to my head

Offended that I made fun of her
Flat chest

But living in the fantasy world
That she had constructed

To deal with the reality
Of living out in the cold

She rambled on—

When your breast size is like mine
You always have to wear a bra...

Then said—
I'm thinking about getting
A breast reduction.

You should, I told her
Then you can get pimples

Then the bowl to the head

And stars
Stars

BROKE DIRECTION

I lived

On the

Streets

So long

They hung

Traffic lights

On my ass

BROKE INTEGRITY AND LITIGATION IN FAST PER SUIT

You have to
Break your neck

To get anywhere
In this country

But I don't
Have the guts

Or a lawyer

BROKE BOHEME

If it weren't for the
   High-heeled calluses
On my feet I would
   Burn myself on all the lit
Cigarette butts people

   Unconsciously flick from
Indifferent fingers
   These here crusty
Swollen kicks
   Are dead ringers

For the real thing
   Even glass can't penetrate
These dead skin clogs
   The most it could do
Is embed itself

   The assortment
Of bottle colors
   Lends a psychedelic
Air of artistic flair
   And the bottle caps

And copper pennies
   Help me cop quarters
As I tap dance my way
   Down the hot shitty
Tambourine streets

BROKE DIAGNOSIS

I have been told by some
That I'm schizophrenic
Because I've gone so long
Without food that sandwiches
Steaks and lamb chops
Sometimes appear to me in mirages
As apparitions

I have been told by some
That I may be a bit paranoid as well
Ever since the mayor
Made it illegal to sleep
In the subway they say
I've never been the same

They didn't believe me
When I told them that an army
Of ants lifted me
From the platform as I slept
And tipped me over
Onto the third rail
As my dream drank the sounds
And sensations of an
On-coming train

I mean they wouldn't
Even believe me
When I suggested that
The ants may be
On the mayor's payroll

To think I always deliberately avoided
Stepping on the motherfuckers
Shhiiiiiit, I could go an extra day or two
On chocolate-covered ants!

BROKE DISH

Life is an ox and a moron
When times are good

I'm doing bad
When I'm doing good

Times are bad
Must be the economic

Conditioners
Tangled up in folks' hair

And times are getting worse
People are looking

At me with less and less contempt
There was a time that they would

Bark at me to get my cup
Out of their face

And to stop looking pitiful
And get a job

But now they too look pitiful
They too have no job

And what I once took as a look
Of contempt may now be

Misconstrued as sympathetic
But I've learned to read faces

My eyes know the seductive look
Of one pleading

Don't get me wrong I'm no psychic
You won't catch me

On TV with my hand on a Bible
Hugged up with Dionne Warwick

I put my faith in reality
Besides the knife and fork

And lobster bib doesn't keep me guessing
I know when someone wants me

For my body

BROKE VALUE

Life is full
Of irony

These days
I've acquired

Use value
This is a feat

For someone
Who lives

On his feet
And who was

Called
All his life

Useless
But now

Conditions being
What they are

People chase me
Down the street

To make use
Of my meat

While
Their children

Wait 'til
I'm asleep

To turn me
Into a

Blowtorch
Or lift me

Off the bench
And turn

My back
Into a

Snow sled

BROKE FAITH

By the time
You decide

To drop
A quarter

In my cup
I'll be

Brushing
My teeth

In a jar

BROKE TOOF

You know
You're

In trouble
When

You're
Missing

A tooth
In your

False teeth

BROKE DENTAL INSURANCE

You have to be careful
When you go to some

Of these dentists
They are shiesty

I fell asleep and they
Took out all of my teeth

And replaced them
With golf tees

BROKE IN PURGATORY

News travels fast
And so does the
New York City
Subterranean circus

Being homeless
And without a TV
May cause the Average Joe
Great misery

In this town
A home and a TV
Is the difference between
Heaven and Hell

But if you live in subway cars
It has its advantages
Although there's no bread
You have all the circus you need

On any given day you may hear:
My name is Cookie
And I'm homeless;
If you could help me out

With some change
So I could get something
To eat, I would
Appreciate it.

And before you know it
Another homeless voice
Yells out:
I could help you out

With some vomit!
And as he is saying this
Another man in the procession
Walks in from the next car

Singing:
My name is Crumb
And I needs some
Not to feel crummy!

I don't mean to be rude
I don't mean to be crude
But I need some clean clothes
Not to feel bummy!

BROKE DAYDREAM

It's not that I
Don't see the stars
Darting out
About my eyes
As you choke me

With your nightstick
And that I refuse to
Shoo them away like flies
Drunk off the fumes
Of horseshit

Or the persistence
Of pesky gnats
My hands cuffed
Behind my back
With your knee

Forcing my ribs
Through the slats
Of this park bench
May have something to do
With my lack of enthusiasm

But let me not go on
Making excuses for my
Immediate reality
The real reason why you don't
See me smiling has less to do

With you choking me or
Trying to wrest a clump of bread
From a pigeon's mouth
And more to do with
Transcontinental outer-body

Daydream time traveling
For a brief minute
I thought I was
In another time
In another place

Kneeling before the guillotine
Watching my head
Roll off into the basket
Of bread I tried to steal
For my children

BROKE COSTUME

Even though I wear the
Same clothes each day
And have
No way
To wash them
Or myself
I'm still invited
To parties
Why just last Halloween
I went to one
Completely naked
Save for a
Colostomy bag
I caught people
Completely off guard
They thought
I couldn't
Afford a costume
That I would be
My usual self
They thought
I would come
As a bum
They weren't
Even close
I had them fooled
You should've seen
The look
On their faces
As they asked
What was I dressed as
And I told them
A bag of shit

BROKE MAN MARCH

Recently
I was asked
If I went to
The Million
Man March

Quite frankly
To be honest
I had my own
Million Man March
With roaches and

Ants and rats
And other vermin
Protesting the
Decrease
Of crumbs
In our neighbor
Hood

We gathered
Together to
Fight the crack-
Heads
Who keep
Dipping into our
Stash

BROKE COMPASSION

You would think the way
I've been treated I would
Strike out with venom

At the sight of a roach
Upside down on the pavement
Especially since I've been

Flipped like a pizza
By a team of them
A few times in my day

Imagine ending up
In the tunnel of a subway
On the third rail

With the headlights of an
On-coming train waking you up
Each night

But I understand
They have it rough too
No low-income housing

No bulletproof welfare cheese
Or anorexic turkey dinners
Don't get me wrong

At times I get the urge
To tap one of them over
Like an armchair and watch

Them crawl and scrape
Frantically across the
Rough shitty pavement

To teach 'em not to fuck
With me
But I'm no sadist

I don't get pleasure
From seeing someone suffer
And I know there are times

When times get so hard
They can't help but to get wasted
And trip up pissy drunk

On all six legs only to land
On the hard shell of their backs
In a twisted frenzied cancan

Plea to get back on their feet
In order to breathe again
And since I have nothing

Else to do but to sit
On the bottom lip
Of the staircase

Of this subway station
Trying to make music
In my gut with the music

Of my cup
I'll sacrifice my sounds
To protect the little scary bastard

Upside down on the ground
Drawing crowds with his clumsy
Palpitating karmic paranoid

Break dance convulsions
Assuring him all the while
That I won't let anyone step

On him
Besides I don't like footprints
On my food

BROKE SHOES

Saving up
Enough money is
Hard enough
As it is

Without
Having to
Cash in
Your ribcage
To get some
Thing to eat

Now they're
Asking me
To give up
My tin can
Shoes
For a mere
Five cents
A piece

I know
These
Thick-ass
Calluses
And these
bunions
Is worth more
Than that

BROKE THANKSGIVING

Sometimes
I lose track of
Time
Days peel by
Like flakes of
Skin

To keep up
And to compensate
I mark time
By the coming
Holidays
Watching

The shoppers
In their frantic search
For gifts and for food
Like for instance
I know it's
Thanksgiving

When I get hungry
And misty-eyed
At the sight
Of Hard lumps
Of dog shit
Laid out here

Next to me
On the curb
Like rolls of stuffed
Sweat socks that remind
Me of the candy yams
My mama used to make

TONY MEDINA

105

BROKE CLARITY

I want to dispel rumors
That homeless people
Are all a bunch
Of lazy drunks who
Spend their days
Sleeping and their nights
Begging for money to get high

To tell you the truth
I don't even drink
I can't take the stuff
It beats my body down
Something worse
Than this shit we
Live under

But you couldn't tell
A few weeks ago
When I could've sworn
I was either drunk or
Needed glasses
I thought I might have to
Play out a scene from *Papillon*

And bust up some Coke bottles
And be like Dustin Hoffman
Hobbling about with thick-ass bifocals
Bumping into trees, walking into swamps
I could've sworn
Some freaky shit
Was going on

At the neighborhood
Whorehouse—
I couldn't believe
What I was seeing—

People dressed up in robes
Swinging incense, ringing bells
And flinging water

But recent events have led me to
Believe that my eyesight
Is as good as ever—
I still have my 20-20
Despite my lack of food
And the frequent flyer rates
I get from dizzy spells

Why just the other day
In the Morisania section of the Bronx
New York City police
Closed down a hotel that stood
Adjacent to a Catholic church
And was used as a
House of ill repute

Before the strange comings
And goings were all a blur to me
Which led to a whirl
Of misunderstandings and confusion
But the police
Have once again managed to
Make things clear to me

Now I can tell which is the church
And which is the ho' house!

BROKE FURNISHINGS

When I was courting
    My first wife
And brought her home
    To my lovely
Refrigerator box

She sat and
    Commented
On my only
    Piece of
Furniture:

Do you think that dictionary's
    Big enough?
I bought that when
    I was a teenager
I wanted to know
    Every word in the world
Really?

No ... . Just:
    FUCK YOU BASTARDS—
LEAVE ME ALONE!
    Which is all I need to know
When the cops come!

BROKE ANECDOTE

You can
Rest assured

That I
Would never

Utter these
Words—

A petite bourgeois
Freak accident

Just occurred
To me:

*The button
On my silk*

*Boxer shorts
Popped off*

*As I
Squat*

*To take
A crap*

BROKE CHRISTMAS

I don't know
I could sit here
And lie to you

And tell you how I saw
That fat white mother—
Climbing out some chimney

Hauling ass in the sky
On the back of some red-nosed reindeer
Bragging about how

He left some shit
For people who already
Got shit

But why lie
You might think
I'm pulling your leg

Or that I'm crazy
Or better yet—
That I'm telling a tall tale

From a short bottle to
Amuse you into
Dropping a coin or

Two into my cup
But I won't allow myself to
Get paid off of telling no lies

To tell you the truth
That fat drunk fuck
Was a landlord or

Bill collector or social worker
(The Ghosts of Christmas
Past Present and Future

Making shit disappear in thin air
And reappear in their pockets!)
He was hauling shit

Out somebody's window
Onto the fire escape
Where three propellered rats

Named The Mimmy Jimmy, The Puta Sucia
And The St. Mary's Baptist Church Choir
Anxiously waited for him

And his bankbook
And rent receipts
And insurance papers and safe

I would've said something
Sooner but the flames
From the burning

Building kept me nice and toasty
Allowing me to roast the heels of my
Boots into marshmallows

Shit, where I come from
When it comes to heat in the winter
It's catch as catch can!

BROKE MAKEOVER AND MISDEMEANOR

They say God works in
Mysterious ways
I would believe this
'Cause getting work has
Always been a mystery to me
But what I want to know is

How He got that job
Where He got it and
Who gave it to Him—
So I can believe even more
'Cause I've been looking
For a job for so long

My corns started looking good to me
Until I was fortunate enough to be
Discovered by a young
White liberal producer of a
Popular television talk show
Who thought it would be

Interesting and cute
To take me off the street
And give me a makeover
Where once I had the
Democratic right to
Starve myself to death

And would've been deemed
An obsessive compulsive
Paranoid schizophrenic
With multiple personalities
And be arrested for impersonating
Three nuns at a Bar Mitzvah

This time, fresh and clean
And spanking brand new
Decked out in new threads
And kicks under the rubric
Of not a makeover show
But a reunion show

(Reunited with life, that is)
I step out the studio doors
And back onto the curb
And get arrested
For impersonating
A human

BROKE BIRTHDAY

Back in the day
When I lost everything
Plus the shirt on my back
Streaking was the big craze

I was a trendsetter
It was fashionable to
Go around in your
Birthday suit

Even when it wasn't
Your birthday
But as time passed me by
Along with the many trucks and cars

That farted out car exhaust
As I stood around
Waiting for handouts
Or windshield wiping gigs

My birthday suit
Literally turned to soot
It got to the point where
I was no longer naked

But was all draped in black
Nearly from head to toe
Taking confessions on
Street corners and at

Under paths
Along the expressway
I became a completely
New man

Mornings I would mourn
My own passing
I was awake
At my own wake

When spring or summer
Rolled along
I would sweat
Something fierce

To which I became
The Invisible Man

BROKE JURISDICKTION

The landlord who evicted me
With propane gas and flames
Copped a plea for arson
And insurance fraud

During trial and after
Under oath and before
The cameras, when asked
Why he did it, and if he
Felt any remorse,
He said: *It was a night*
At the races — I took a gamble
And lost

It was a shame the judge
Didn't throw the book at him
For being so evil and arrogant
That he brought marshmallows
To the low-income bonfire.

I would've loved to bring
Marshmallows to his electrocution
But the judge gave him a slap
On the wrist and later took him out
For drinks to celebrate.

BROKE TIP

If you
Find your

Self in a
Restaurant

Or a diner
And the waiter

Brings you
A bowl

Of soup
With a

Fly
In it

Make
Sure

He doesn't
Charge

You
Extra

BROKE IN LONDON

In London
It rains
All the time
The fog's
So thick

You have
To unzip it
So you could
Leave your
House

You have
To have
The sun
Federal Expressed
To you

It shows up
As often
As the insurance man
Or your
Welfare check

BROKE STORM WARNING IN EFFECT

I should have known
That when I married you
I'd need a crash helmet

I didn't expect
To have a ceiling fan
In my soup

My mother warned me
About your cooking
But you keep saying

She's against you –
She never liked you
In the first place

She warned me about
Your cooking
But you keep blaming it

On El Niño
I should have listened to her
That night before

Our wedding
She told me
I'd be back

First chance
I get

BROKE BONOBO

We were separated
By a river
She was busy
And wouldn't even
Give me a slither
Of banana peel
Although I appealed
To her sense of matriarchy
I said, *Cut the malarkey* —
Give me a piece of that
'Nana — it's not like
I'm asking for much
Or manna — by jiminy
It's hard out here
For a chimp
In the jungle
With no chimney
Swinging from branch
To branch defending
Your honor —
She said, *Do me*
A solid, babe
And fetch me some
Junglesop —
To which I
Snorted and plodded
And clopped about
To make her happy
We spent that night
Wearing out our
Copy of the Karma Sutra,
Bending branches,
Shaming leaves
At one point
I caught a draft
And sneezed —
Blowing the whole
Damn thing —

All I wanted to do
Was sing
Let her in on
What I was feeling
But she was no longer
In the mood
And I tried not
To brood
Besides, the moon
Hung so low
I climbed up
On its crescent
And spent the night
In the crook of
Its glow
While she snored
And snored,
Talking about me
In her sleep, sucking
Her teeth, mumbling –
This motherfucker...

BROKE ON VIAGRA

After reading *The Joy of Sex*
For I don't know how many times

She wanted to mount the kitchen table
Or the top of the refrigerator

And jump on top
Of me—

She wanted to break me off
Without breaking me off

That's why I think she spiked
My morning coffee

But was upset when up
From my morning paper

All I could raise beside
My right hand

With its favorite cup
Was an eyebrow

BROKE VIAGRA FALLS

It used to be
That you
Would find
Yourself

Down and out
And without
A helping hand
Or a prayer

In the world
And end up
In Niagara Falls
Going over

In a barrel
Trying to
End it all

Now
If your wife
Can't get
You hard

Or you lost
All contact
And communication
With your person—

Fuck Niagara Falls!
You're going out
The window
Wall Street
Stock Market Crash style

Headfirst
In a bucket
Of sleeping pills

TONY MEDINA

123

BROKE DRONES

I was stung by so many bees
　　My face bees looking like a
Pomegranate taken for granted

Laying out in the sun too long—
　　What I get for falling asleep
On flowered concrete beneath

A cherry blossom tree
　　Only to be wakened by
Drones buzzing about my

Retractable hairline and
　　Moses-on-mescaline-back-from-
Burning-some-bush beard—bees

Buzzing in and out my ears like
　　Government spies planting
Microchips—bees tracking

And retracting in and out
　　Like my ear was a honeycomb
Waxing beesological on how

Fortunate it is that I haven't
　　Cleaned my ears in so long
They may—at best—discover

Another planet in there and—at
　　The very least—Jimmy Hoffa's bones
As they bump about and drone

To the tune of my put-put-puttering
　　Breathing with its own warbled
Tone and lazy snore-wracked drone

BROKE KARMA

Wasn't sizzurp
That seized

Lil Wayne
By the throat

But the ghost
Of Emmett Till

Beatin' his thang
Of a soul up

BROKE FOR BEGINNERS

I used to moonlight as moonshine
Now I moonlight as moonlight

My kicks were outta sight
Now they are out of sight

Snatched off by some punks
Playing a practical joke

Or some jailhouse freak
Selling them back to me for smokes

Better not catch no
Sewer rat rockin' 'em

End up dried-out crunchy crisp
And tased on the third rail

How my hair wound up
A bird's nest

Is anybody's guess—
Drugs war poverty

Despair—who cares
When one has bigger problems

Like worrying about food
To eat with no fish to fry

In the beginning was
The hunger and the wail

Then came Cain dissing Abel
Murder death sin blues and taxes

Absent father gone to get a pack
Angry mother an emotional ransack

Prison guards and jail—the deck is stacked
Like I said, It's a fact—I used to moonlight

As moonshine, carefree as light crinkling
On water—now I moonlight as midnight

Humping trashcans for what's discarded
Without no son or daughter

BROKE BETTER RECOGNIZE

This girl was walking down
The street and this guy said,

Aye, baby, you are so sexy.
Can I holler at you?

She ignored him and, as she
Passed him by, he yelled, *Bitch!*

She turned around and said,
Hey, motherfucker!

How did you
Know my name?

And he said, *Oh shit!*
How did you know my name?

BROKE BACK MOUNTAIN

She was spotted by the eyes of the frozen foods manager stuffing ham hocks and hog maws in her bra. He abducted her before she could slip a couple of hams up her dress and fasten them to her belly with a three-foot sausage link. He had her cough up the goods into the sink of one of the backrooms where meat hung raw and red like the open wailing mouth of a baby frozen in mid-scream. Snatching off her wig, he grimaced at the sight of sardine cans shifting and sliding and avalanching off her wispy noggin, nearly taking off his kneecap and straightening out her bunions. *Lift up your arms,* he told her. The flabs concealed onions. Oh god, he thought, holding his breath, fanning the fumes with his lashes. But the whiff of the onions proved to be too overwhelming for the manager. Before he knew it, he was on the floor breakdancing and gasping for air. The big woman started to make a break for it, running toward the plastic strips hanging in the doorway. She turned back to what seemed like another attempt to snatch a ham, but suddenly changed her mind. She knelt over the frail manager's jerky, convulsing body, and before he could twitch himself into a never-ending coma, clutching his lower back in agony, laid her big lips on him, giving him mouth-to-mouth. Before his eyes could focus in on hers, she snatched him up under her arm and headed through the aisles like a running back.

BROKE LIGHT MOTIF

I'm
So broke

The only
Light

I have
In my apartment

Is a
Laser gun

Sight

BROKE QUESTION OF THE DAY

Is it because
I have

No money
To lay out

For campaign
Contributions

That I'm forced
To lay out

On the street?

BROKE TONY BENNETT

I left my heart
In San Francisco

And a lung
And a couple of ribs

That were
Attached

Some kneecaps
Maybe

Blood on a
Nightstick

My right eye on the
Tip of a baton

Wielded by cops
They must've

Shipped in from a
Rodney King cattle call

In East LA
Propositioning to deal

187 more
Death blows

Just for the record
Before the year is out

BROKE JOAN RIVERS

Oh, grow up!
  Can we talk?

Oof – that hair!
  So Baroque!

It looks like an inverted
  Vaulted ceiling dipped

In marmalade
  With wrinkles on top

If that dress was any tighter
  Her date would be having

Chiffon spare ribs for dinner
  She squeezes any more feet

Into that shoe, the red carpet
  Is going to look like it's being

Humped by Vienna sausages
  She had so much plastic surgery

Her doctor's on standby
  To do Botox touchups

Her face looks like a
  Samsonite trunk

You can't
  Quite shut

TONY MEDINA

133

BROKE PLAYER

Reporter:

How many children

Do you have, Travis?

Travis Henry

(Former NFL

Running Back):

I got 9.

Reporter:

With how many

Different women?

Travis Henry:

9.

BROKE HEADLINE NEWS

Fast Food Worker
Stabs Customers

In Argument Over
Botched Order: Police

I would expect
This sort of heinous

Knife attack
From the taco beef

Pork or chicken – Not
The fast food worker!

BROKE RECIPE

Cobwebs and dust
        Glass and pus
Marinate with
        Hot air from
A street grate
        Sautee in rain
Sleet and snow
        Sprinkle subway
Soot and pigeon
        Shit crumbs
And dirty bubblegum
        Embedded in tar
And concrete stuck
        To the bottom of a shoe
Let bake in the noon
        Day sun and cool
In the open air
        Sewer fumes of the street
Like a flesh wound
        Serve up with a
Discarded crust
        Dipped in
Leftover beer
        Dribbles from
An empty can
        Bon appetit

BROKE PLACES I'VE LIVED

I've lived in apartments the size of glove compartments
Evicted from my flesh by nightsticks and government

Sanctioned bomb squad fire departments
I've lived on the steps of churches with big doors

And crooked steeples with priests who cared
More about pubescence than poor people

I've slept on street graters in front of the White House
While diplomats and tourists circumnavigated my

Cardboard silhouette in search of the best
Angle for their drive-by snapshot Russian Roulette

I've slept along railroad tracks 'til dawn
In freight cars where I was born

To cover myself in hay to keep warm
Or go unnoticed and jump off where I please

Barnyard animals pelted me with feed
Cows belted me with their knees

I've never owned a real set of keys
Even monkeys hurled shit at me

At the zoo where hyenas would boo
And shoo me away

I've lived in places I could not stay
In places too expensive to pay

Where I wouldn't be forced to wash dishes
But where I'd be a human squeegee scraped across

Moving windshields wiping blood and snot
And flies from my toothless smile-less

TONY MEDINA

137

Bugged-out eyes
I've lived on reservations without reservation

In war zones where I was too zoned to realize
The war was being conducted

In my underwear by irate
Ticks and fleas on the warpath

I've lived in skin as hard as Samsonite bags
Bones as stiff and brittle as day-old bread

I've lived the life of the dead
For most of my days

Most of my days

BROKE TEA PARTIES AND REENLISTMENT

They repossessed my ribcage
Lugged around my lungs
Like luggage
Went bowling with my skull
A thumb in the mouth, a
Finger in each nostril—
Strike! Pinned between
The lane and the gutter,
I contemplated tea
Parties and massacres.
My mascara ran down
My face like a Lone Ranger mask.
Voted me into the Raccoon
Lodge. Learned a
New hat shake. Shook
A tail feather with a
Banana skirt, put it on
Like a lampshade, after a
Dry martini or two, shook
My hips like maracas, cuchi
Cuchi like Charo like Chiquita
Banana like Josephine Baker,
Ear we go again, same old
Shit again, marching
Down the avenue,
Two more days
And we'll be through
Sound off — one, two —
Sound off — three, four —
Break it on down —
One two three four
One two — three four!
Left left Left right
O' left   Right o' left
Right   Left

BROKE BARBIE

Lives in the cardboard box
She came in

Not a Mattel original
Straight off the

Showroom floor
But a factory flung

Bland broken down
Generic one

Face weather-beaten
And worn, her once

Bright smile whittled
Down by the sadness

Of hunger and time
Hair matted

Feet dirty
And covered in

Tiny black disposable
Garbage bags

This Barbie
Been through a lot

This Barbie
Walks the streets

Roams through
Tiny trash bins

In search of meals
This Barbie does not

Have a price tag or a seal
Her cold plastic rubbery skin

Has a grimy film
Like a dirty eraser

You rub to make
Clean again

Her Ken left her
For a crack pipe

So small
You could barely

Hold it with
Two fingers

This Barbie's mama
Put her out

A long time ago
For not doing

What she said
For running behind boys

For staying out
All hours

Of the night
For dropping out of school

For getting knocked up
For aborting twins

For cursing and fighting
For insisting her stepfather

Touched her

BROKE HOMELAND SECURITY

It's getting so hard to
   Say things nowadays

I was in the subway
   And a friend of mine

Says to me, *Let's blow*
   This joint—

And as we were about
   To leave, two big beefy

Brawny cops
   Pounce on us—

Blindsiding us like a
   Cheap shot in a barroom

Brawl—wrestling us to the
   Ground

Pounding our heads into
   Exclamation points

With their wildly wielding
   Wanton batons

Turning our skullcaps into
   Percussion instrument

Sounds of Flintstone knots and
   Stars abound

We tried to explain the
   Situation while hogtied

In the back of the
   Paddy wagon

But the pushy priggish pigs were
    Pugnacious in their pomposity

Refusing to acknowledge our
    Freedom of expiration

BROKE DRESS CODE
(Don't Sweat the Small Stuff)

Don't care much
About no sagging
Jeans like rumpled
Suits on some broke
Down racks

I'm more
Worried
About these
Sagging
Sacks

I lugs around
Like a broke-ass
Santa with no
Reindeer sleigh or
Chimney cracks

BROKE HISTORY OF THE WORLD

They had to kill God
In order to get
The day off

They had to bomb them out
To get them to pay
Their rent

They had to pollute the water
In order to get the fish
To comply

They had to set fire to the trees
To burn you out
Into the open

They had to poison the children
With church and TV
To get them to stop
Singing

And soon more trees disappeared
And water was hard to come by
And the children, well, it

Was hard to keep them
In those prisons
Working for free

BROKE SOLDIER OF FORTUNE

It seems like war
Is a revolving door
I'm caught in its
Unpredictable steel jaw

This is my third tour
They're working me like
A government mule

On my first tour
They cut my benefits
By sixty percent

On my second
The enemy cut
My right leg
By forty

I wonder if my
Prosthetic will melt
By the lightning heat
Of a roadside bomb

I've been here so long
I'm starting to shit
Sand and oil

I guess this is
What they mean
By the spoils
Of war

BROKE SALVATION AND GOOD FORTUNE

When black birds
Do not mistake
Your eyes for
Dried-out pieces
Of fruit

When sex is not spent
On the belly
In rundown cheap
Hotels of Kleenex
Pap smear nights

When your bones
Do not crumble
Under the tug and pull
Of your evaporating
Skin

When your lungs
Are no longer
Dried-up
Cobweb caves
Whistling Dixie

As ants carry you
Off like a game-
Winning football
Spiking you into
Sewers of despair

When what you
Fear most
Is not water
Or food
Or air

TONY MEDINA

147

BROKE BOBBLEHEAD BOP

I drank a tsunami once
Opened the back window of my
Cardboard condo to let some fresh air in
Through its tail—and a rainforest of wind
Bum rushed its way in
Swallowing my Jonah like a whale

I can't stand the rain
> *Against my window*
> *Bringing back sweet memories*

Before I knew it I was knee-deep
In some serious sea salt tsunami spit—no shit!
Two cans of Bustello that was my bathroom
And even my concrete curbside bedroom set
Passed me by—my world reduced to
A sty in the eye—everything in my flapping closets
And cupboards floated away, along with me
Looking like a broke Popsicle stick bobblehead doll

Hey window pane
Do you remember
> *How sweet it used to be*
> *When we were together*

My whole cul-de-sac—bum rushed and ransacked—
Was a water world whirlpool of shocked and awed neighbors
Gurgling and flapping and floundering about for a boat, trying to stay
Afloat with tree branches, rats, tire irons, park bench
Hunks and cardboard chunks—even rattlesnakes and skunks—
While others slept soundly in their bunks

Everything was so grand
Now that we've parted

> *There's just one sound*
> *That I just can't stand*

BROKE LINT IN A WALLET

I try to keep my
    Bones wet and
My skin warm
    And wrapped
Around some
    Veins

Keeping my
    Blood in
But I have
    Leaks

And my skin
    Speaks
Dry dust
    Floating off
My bones

    I've been
Reduced to
    Lint
Sandwiched
    Between
Some credit
    Cards

BROKE BALLOT

I vote for triage units for teachers
Free pork chops for preachers
Soft concrete for homeless to sleep
I vote for the equal distribution of surplus cheese
I vote for Spam to be designated a vegetable
For more housing projects elevator pee
I vote for the Statue of Liberty to get down on one knee
I vote for the rich to always win the lottery
Of despair
I vote for Satan to get a new Halloween costume
And The Pope to bust out a couple of breakdance moves
I vote for Rush Limbaugh to never get that Vicodin bottle out his ass
I vote for Ann Coulter to come out as a reptilian cross dresser
I vote for the resurrection of that Renaissance painting of Jesus
Smoking grass and beating money-changing mofos with his
Sandals for their cash
I vote for Viagara to be given out like communion wafers in Congress
I vote for more air laced with plumes of dope
And water that resembles chunky soup
I vote for hurricanes to be rerouted to the mansions of the rich
And war rooms to be reduced to a ditch
I vote for poor people to snitch out the rich like kids who catch
their siblings with their hands in the cookie jar
I vote for a country that stinks but does not itch
For clogged arteries and high fructose corn syrup tears
I vote for Budweiser beer for breakfast
No tread marks in my cereal or
Flags sticking out my ass
At half-staff

BROKE RAPPER

Two turntables
And a microphone

To me
Involves garbage can lids
And a toothless comb

When it rains
I look like a

West Coast rapper
With a sopping
Jheri curl weave

The kind that leaves
Grease stains wherever it please

With hair like this you could
Never commit a crime
As serious as murder

CSI would have
A field day

With all that nasty
Evidence you'd
Leave behind

You'd be so busy trying to
Mop up blood

When what you need
To be worrying about is
The mop under that baseball cap

There was a time when I
Used to think having

TONY MEDINA

151

Diamond-encrusted dentures
Was the shiznick
And wearing my pants

Hanging off the cliff of my ass
Was fly

And had all the girls
Batting their eyes
Now I can't keep

The flies out my
Exposed crack

And the girls can't
Open their eyes
Enough to bat their lashes

For the stench poking them
Giving them a sty

And when I try to rhyme
I can't hold the mic
Without having to

Yank my droopy drawers
Up

So to me
Being a rapper
Means having messed up hair

A broke toothless comb
And all assed out

BROKE FAIR EXCHANGE

You Pop-Tart
    You Fruity Pebbles

You tricks are for kids
    You tore up lobster bib

You Limoncello
    You shaking Jello

You candelabra
    You piano cantata

You Lysol spray
    You smoking ashtray

You Nipsey Russell
    You tipsy with no hustle

You broke bitch itch
    You low-down snitch

You back scratch
    You purse snatch

You two-time loser
    You back street boozer

You one-eyed jack
    You break your mama's back

You rude end of a pimp smack
    You Dunkin' Donuts heart attack

You schoolyard simp
    You wrist with a limp

You cockeyed Rubik's Cube
    You contaminated condom lube

You Pepto Bismol
   You look so dismal

You salmonella
   You nasty fella

You asparagus tip
   You busted lip

You dumb mofo
   You broke back ho'

You incongruous whore
   You open sore sewer

BROKE ODE

To the hole in the shoe
To the sock drenched in puddle drool

To the leak that can't be plugged
To the ceiling mimicking the sky

To winter nights in wine bottles getting high
To cracks in the wall to store all that you are

To not being able to get that far
To the shopping cart's twisted heel

To the sun bending on one knee
To the wind slapping you around like a thin tree

To the cool breeze letting you know you're alive
To the cobwebs in the ribcage you despise

To the human face you wear as a disguise
To the invisibility of subway car rides

To walking aimlessly down cold cobblestone hides
To the dry rumbling in each lung

To the sound of the pinball machine when you were young
To the good old days when food was not scarce

To the warm breast milk of your mother's care
To the rainwater that pours down in a shower

To the bus that passes you by
To the splash that stabs you in the eye

To the empty belch echo that never strays
To the hunger pangs banging out a clave

TONY MEDINA
155

BROKE HELLUVA TOWN

Vacant lot eyes
Slumped abandoned building of flesh
Rail thin clothesline of dry skin
Draped in black disposable plastic bag
Stuffed with scraps of yesterday's news

In a cardboard pup tent
On street grater street corner grime
The heat of the city rising up
Like dog breath or what passes through bowels
The wind is a torturer's apprentice

Whistling and taunting mercilessly
Like a prizefighter sticking and moving
Between each creak of bone
Cold curing skin into soft leather creases
Across concrete canvas of asphalt flesh

In frozen mouth of piss puddle rain
What rats will gnaw at me at night
What young street toughs will douse me
With lighter fluid while I sleep
And resurrect me

As flame

BROKE "It Is What It Is"

My voice was golden
When I spoke velvet-winged doves
Emerged from it like lavender lava
From the pouting lips of Mount Vesuvius
This was the gift the gods had intoned on me
My mother proud to hear hints of the possibility
Of my long dead father her husband baritoning
From the sweet tea kettle of her dreams
Whenever I spoke or my voice wafted into open rooms
Brooms would come to a sweeping halt
People would stop in their tracks
Objects levitated just above the space they were placed
Mama had high hopes for my golden pipes and me
But then I played Russian roulette with what the good Lord had
Given me and ended up introducing my lips to a different pipe
Fame and fortune exchanging places with the residue and ash of my misery
I left my wife and kids; I cut my mama off and the rest of my kin
I descended into a hellhole of self-indulgent sin
Until my life was an empty broke bottle of gin
In the back alley piss puddle of a dead dick dog
Down on his luck so bad even his bark was broke
And his bite was a poke—in my ribs
I got kicked out of so many cribs I walked around the streets
With nothing but a big-ass geometric 'fro and lobster bib
The 'fro grew so out of control squirrels looked for nuts in there
While pigeons perched and shat everywhichawhere
People thought I had a nest for a hat
Children came to visit and point at what they thought were robin eggs
Then one day I made a cardboard sign that said *Will Speak for Food*
A reporter found me on the side of a road and videotaped me
Flapping my golden chops for change
My story made the Internet go insane
With people wondering—*What the hell?*
And everyone wanted me to yell—for money
Until I made the morning talk show rounds and life
Became a revolving door of people pulling me here there and
Everywhere, throwing money at me as if it were rice
And I were its groom

TONY MEDINA
157

I was all over the place and more recognizable
Than George Washington on a dollar bill
     It got so bad I got ill I could not think and needed to rest
My weary feet and soak them in a vat of beer
     'Til—in it—the rest of me did sink
As the limos they sent for me drove me to drink

ACKNOWLEDGMENTS

Grateful acknowledgment is made to the editors of the following journals, anthologies, websites, exhibits and books, where versions of these poems first appeared:

An Onion of Wars by Tony Medina (Third World Press, 2012), "Broke Found Poem" and "Broke Barbie"

Little Patuxent Review, Social Justice (Issue 11, Winter 2012), "Broke Ode" and "Broke 'It Is What It Is',"

Paterson Literary Review (PLR) #37 (2009), "Broke Barbie"

Committed to Breathing by Tony Medina (Third World Press, 2003), "Broke Regrets" and "Broke Success"

Page 141, "Broke Bobblehead Bop": I can't stand the rain/Against my window/Bringing back sweet memories/Hey windowpane/Do you remember/How sweet it used to be/When we were together/Everything was so grand/Now that we're parted/There's just one sound/That I just can't stand" is from Tina Turner's "I Can't Stand the Rain," lyrics by Ann Peeples, Don Bryant and Bernard Miller.

I would like to thank Gabrielle David, publisher of 2Leaf Press, for publishing *Broke Baroque,* as well as Team 2Leaf and the Board of Directors of the Intercultural Alliance of Artists & Scholars, Inc., including Naydene Brickus, Angela Sternreich and Stephanie Agosto-Negrón. I would also like to thank Miriam Ahmed for the beautiful cover design, as well as the Estate of Jean-Michel Basquiat and the Artists Rights Society for permission to use Jean-Michel Basquiat's great painting, *Boy and Dog in a Johnnypump,* for the cover of *Broke Baroque.* Sincere thanks to filmmaker Vagabond Beaumont for his great *Broke Baroque* book trailer that can be viewed on 2leafpress.org. Last, but certainly not least, I would like to thank the great Ishmael Reed for his powerful introduction, "Poet Laureate of the Broke." I appreciate all the talent, intelligence and hard work that helped bring this book into the world.

Gabrielle David gets the last word: *Love to the Godmothers!* ❖

ABOUT THE AUTHOR

TONY MEDINA, two-time winner of the Paterson Prize, is the author and editor of seventeen books for adults and young readers, including *De-Shawn Days* (Lee & Low Books, 2001), *Bum Rush the Page: A Def Poetry Jam* (Random House/Three Rivers Press, 2001), *Love to Langston* (Lee & Low Books, 2002), *Committed to Breathing* (Third World Press, 2003) and *Follow-up Letters to Santa from Kids who Never Got a Response* (Just Us Books, 2003). His poetry, fiction, and essays appear in over a hundred publications and several CD compilations. He has taught English at Long Island University's Brooklyn campus and Borough of Manhattan Community College, CUNY, and has earned an MA and PhD in English from Binghamton University, SUNY. The first Professor of Creative Writing at Howard University, Medina's most recent books are *I and I, Bob Marley* (Lee & Low Books), *My Old Man Was Always on the Lam* (NYQ Books), a finalist for the 2011 Paterson Poetry Prize, *Broke on Ice* (Willow Books), *An Onion of Wars* (Third World Press) and *The President Looks Like Me & Other Poems* (Just Us Books). In 2013, he received both the Langston Hughes Society Award and the first African Voices Literary Award. ❖

OTHER BOOKS BY 2LEAF PRESS

2LEAF PRESS challenges the status quo by publishing alternative fiction, non-fiction, poetry and bilingual works by activists, academics, poets and authors dedicated to diversity and social justice with scholarship that is accessible to the general public. 2LEAF PRESS produces high quality and beautifully produced hardcover, paperback and ebook formats through our series: *2LP Explorations in Diversity, 2LP University Books, 2LP Classics, 2LP Translations, Nuyorican World Series,* and *2LP Current Affairs, Culture & Politics.* Below is a selection of 2LEAF PRESS' published titles.

2LP EXPLORATIONS IN DIVERSITY

Substance of Fire: Gender and Race in the College Classroom
by Claire Millikin
Foreword by R. Joseph Rodríguez, Afterword by Richard Delgado
Contributed material by Riley Blanks, Blake Calhoun, Rox Trujillo

Black Lives Have Always Mattered
A Collection of Essays, Poems, and Personal Narratives
Edited by Abiodun Oyewole

The Beiging of America:
Personal Narratives about Being Mixed Race in the 21st Century
Edited by Cathy J. Schlund-Vials, Sean Frederick Forbes, Tara Betts
with an Afterword by Heidi Durrow

What Does it Mean to be White in America?
Breaking the White Code of Silence, A Collection of Personal Narratives
Edited by Gabrielle David and Sean Frederick Forbes
Introduction by Debby Irving and Afterword by Tara Betts

2LP UNIVERSITY BOOKS
Designs of Blackness, Mappings in the Literature and
Culture of African Americans
A. Robert Lee
20TH ANNIVERSARY EXPANDED EDITION

2LP CLASSICS
Adventures in Black and White
Edited and with a critical introduction by Tara Betts
by Philippa Duke Schuyler

Monsters: Mary Shelley's Frankenstein and Mathilda
by Mary Shelley, edited by Claire Millikin Raymond

2LP TRANSLATIONS
Birds on the Kiswar Tree
by Odi Gonzales, Translated by Lynn Levin
Bilingual: English/Spanish

Incessant Beauty, A Bilingual Anthology
by Ana Rossetti, Edited and Translated by Carmela Ferradáns
Bilingual: English/Spanish

NUYORICAN WORLD SERIES
Our Nuyorican Thing, The Birth of a Self-Made Identity
by Samuel Carrion Diaz, with an Introduction by Urayoán Noel
Bilingual: English/Spanish

Hey Yo! Yo Soy!, 40 Years of Nuyorican Street Poetry,
The Collected Works of Jesús Papoleto Meléndez
Bilingual: English/Spanish

LITERARY NONFICTION
No Vacancy; Homeless Women in Paradise
by Michael Reid

The Beauty of Being, A Collection of Fables, Short Stories & Essays
by Abiodun Oyewole

WHEREABOUTS: Stepping Out of Place,
An Outside in Literary & Travel Magazine Anthology
Edited by Brandi Dawn Henderson

PLAYS
Rivers of Women, The Play
by Shirley Bradley LeFlore, with photographs by Michael J. Bracey

AUTOBIOGRAPHIES/MEMOIRS/BIOGRAPHIES
Trailblazers, Black Women Who Helped Make America Great
American Firsts/American Icons
by Gabrielle David

Mother of Orphans
The True and Curious Story of Irish Alice, A Colored Man's Widow
by Dedria Humphries Barker

Strength of Soul
by Naomi Raquel Enright

Dream of the Water Children:
Memory and Mourning in the Black Pacific
by Fredrick D. Kakinami Cloyd
Foreword by Velina Hasu Houston, Introduction by Gerald Horne
Edited by Karen Chau

The Fourth Moment: Journeys from the Known to the Unknown, A Memoir
by Carole J. Garrison, Introduction by Sarah Willis

POETRY
PAPOLíTICO, Poems of a Political Persuasion
by Jesús Papoleto Meléndez
with an Introduction by Joel Kovel and DeeDee Halleck

Critics of Mystery Marvel, Collected Poems
by Youssef Alaoui, with an Introduction by Laila Halaby

shrimp
by jason vasser-elong, with an Introduction by Michael Castro
The Revlon Slough, New and Selected Poems
by Ray DiZazzo, with an Introduction by Claire Millikin

Written Eye: Visuals/Verse
by A. Robert Lee

A Country Without Borders: Poems and Stories of Kashmir
by Lalita Pandit Hogan, with an Introduction by Frederick Luis Aldama

Branches of the Tree of Life
The Collected Poems of Abiodun Oyewole 1969-2013
by Abiodun Oyewole, edited by Gabrielle David
with an Introduction by Betty J. Dopson

2Leaf Press is an imprint owned and operated by the Intercultural Alliance of Artists & Scholars, Inc. (IAAS), a NY-based nonprofit organization that publishes and promotes multicultural literature.

NEW YORK
www.2leafpress.org